When the Money Runs Out

Hope and Help for
the Financially Stressed

James C. Petty

New
Growth
Press

www.newgrowthpress.com

New Growth Press, Greensboro, NC 27404
Copyright © 2009 by James C. Petty
All rights reserved. Published 2009.

Typesetting: Robin Black, www.blackbirdcreative.biz

ISBN-10: 1-935273-05-1
ISBN-13: 978-1-935273-05-9

Library of Congress Cataloging-in-Publication Data

Petty, James C., 1944-
 When the money runs out : hope and help for the financially stressed / James Chalmers Petty.
     p. cm. — (Resources for personal change)
 Includes bibliographical references and index.
 ISBN-13: 978-1-935273-05-9
 ISBN-10: 1-935273-05-1
 1. Trust in God—Christianity. 2. Wealth—Religious aspects—Christianity. 3. Money—Religious aspects—Christianity. I. Title.
 BV4637.P48 2009
 248.8'6—dc22

                                    2009016569

Printed in Canada
19 18 17 16 15 14 13 12   4 5 6 7 8

Shannon and Jeff have three children and own their own home. Jeff is a sales manager, and Shannon works part time as a nurse. Six months ago their mortgage payments went up, and now they are having trouble paying their bills. At the end of each month, they look at each other and wonder where all the money went. Some nights it's hard to sleep—they are afraid they will end up losing their home.

Richard worked for thirty years as an engineer for a computer company. His company survived many economic crises, but it didn't survive this last one. He was laid off last week and is now on unemployment. He lies awake at night worrying about his large home-equity loan payment, what he should do next, and how his family will cope with their sudden decrease in income.

Tamara and Andy just got married and are both still in college. They are working part time and borrowing money to pay their tuition. They have just enough to live on, so if they have an unexpected expense they put it on their credit card. Now Tamara is expecting a baby. They're happy, but also anxious. How will they make ends meet now?

Fearful . . . worried . . . anxious . . . those are some of the ways people typically respond to financial stress.

There are many reasons people struggle financially—job loss, unexpected expenses, poor decisions—but, whatever the reason, money troubles are serious, painful, and stressful. If you are experiencing financial difficulties, you might be feeling anger, discouragement, fear, or even panic.

When you are financially stressed, it is easy to become consumed by your worries and fears. Jesus knows this, so he reminds us not to "set your heart on what you will eat or drink; do not worry about it. For the pagan world runs after all such things, and your Father knows that you need them. But seek his kingdom, and these things will be given to you as well. Do not be afraid, little flock, for your Father has been pleased to give you the kingdom" (Luke 12:29–32).

In the midst of all the different emotions and fears you have about your finances, start by simply reminding yourself every day that your heavenly Father already knows what you need. So instead of being consumed by your financial problems, you can "set your heart" on the most valuable thing in the world—knowing Jesus and being a part of his kingdom. He is the one who brings us true life, not our jobs, our bank accounts, or our material possessions. The apostle John put it this way: "He who has the Son has life; he who does not have the Son of God does not have life" (1 John 5:12).

Like many people, I had to learn these lessons the hard way as I faced my own financial meltdown. Many years ago, I was a young pastor, married with three small children, and had just started a new church. My wife Marsha and I couldn't seem to make ends meet on my church planter's salary. In one year we spent twenty percent more than I earned! Facing that reality filled me with fear and embarrassment. After all, wasn't I the one who was supposed to be a role model to the families in my church? I felt like a failure.

But God used our financial struggles to refocus our lives on him and to grow and change us. Financial problems, like all of life's struggles, are not random events, but trials that God allows so we become more like him. Jesus describes this as "pruning" that results in us bearing more fruit (John 15:1–3). Through the years, God has given Marsha and me many opportunities to be "pruned" through financial struggles. It has never been easy nor felt great, but God has been with us every step of the way.

So take heart: your financial troubles take place in the larger story of our all-powerful God's plan to redeem you in and through your unique trials. In fact, your financial trials provide the opportunity for God to change you in ways you would never trade for all the money in the world!

An Opportunity to Gain the True Wealth of Contentment

One way that God wants to grow all of us is in the area of contentment. True contentment is usually learned on the down cycle—in loss, deprivation, and financial need. As your own dreams of financial security are shaken by your circumstances, you have the opportunity to turn from trusting and hoping in material things to trusting and hoping in God. This might not seem so great right now, but think about it: if your contentment is based on what you have or own, it can be easily lost. But contentment based on your relationship with God is on the unshakeable ground of God's unfailing love.

The apostle Paul explains it like this: "I have learned to be content whatever the circumstances. I know what it is to be in need, and I know what it is to have plenty. I have learned the secret of being content in any and every situation, whether well fed or hungry, whether living in plenty or in want. I can do everything through him who gives me strength" (Philippians 4:11–13).

Paul is saying that true contentment (or lack of it) doesn't come from our circumstances; true contentment comes from "him who gives me strength." Because he trusted Jesus, he was at peace in all kinds of material circumstances. He knew that even in times of financial stress he was not missing out on anything essential to life. His identity, hope, and well-being did not come from what he owned or what goal he achieved. Rather, it rested on his relationship with his heavenly Father, who loved him and gave his Son for him.

Before this financial crisis hit, you might not have realized how much of your hope, contentment, and sense of well-being was attached to your earning power, your possessions, and your bank balance. So don't be discouraged as you struggle with these common issues. Instead, do these four things:

1. *Ask yourself whether you really want God-centered contentment.* Many times we want contentment, but only on the terms and circumstances dictated by us. Turning to God in times of loss and learning to let go of these requirements is

deeply challenging, but the first step toward true contentment.

2. *Identify what you fear losing or what you believe you need for happiness.* Then ask God to help you give these things to him and trust him to supply all your needs in Christ Jesus.

3. *When you notice you are discontented, ask God to forgive you for Jesus' sake.* Don't be discouraged if you need to do this every hour! Jesus promises forgiveness and the grace to change to those who come to him in repentance (1 John 1:9).

4. *Cultivate a sense of your phenomenal wealth in the Father of Jesus Christ.* He is your God, your refuge, your treasure, your true inheritance, and your portion forever. Meditate on your "wealth" in Ephesians 1:3–23 or many of the Psalms (i.e. Psalm 62; 63; 65; 73).

When our treasure is in our relationship with Christ, then we, like Paul, can be freed *from* seeking life in the things that we possess, and freed *to* actually live in the fallen real world and remain in the Living Branch that bears fruit for eternity (John 15:5).

Godly contentment has a powerful bearing on our adaptability. It powers our ability to successfully flex our lifestyle downwards without despair or upwards without pride should God grant us economic success. God-centered contentment guards us from becoming prisoners of what we own or the lifestyle we enjoy. It protects us from regret about what we don't have or haven't achieved. Lastly it guards us from being pierced by the "many griefs" that come from the pursuit of riches (1 Timothy 6:10).

Godliness with contentment truly is great gain (1 Timothy 6:6).

An Opportunity to Examine What Money Means to You

As you think through your struggles with contentment, you will start to notice the meaning and value you have attached to money. So this is another opportunity for growth and change in your life. Here are some of the more common values attached to money:

- Providing safety and security
- Providing validation in the competition of life
- Providing power to control people and circumstances

- Giving enjoyment, pleasure, and comfort
- Enabling us to impress others (with what we own, how we look, etc.)
- Enabling us to please those we care about (i.e. children, spouse, parents, friends)
- Enabling us to identify with a particular group

A recent article by a financial writer made a similar list of the different values people attach to money.[1] It is interesting that the list did not even offer the possibility of the value God places on money—to be a means by which we bless and give to others.

Attaching this value to money never emerges from the natural human heart. Our values emerge from our particular personality, life experiences, and family background. But no matter what value you attach to money, if you're relying on money to provide you with security, identity, comfort, and purpose, you are using money to find life apart from God.

Then money (or the lack of it) can easily become the secret "mistress" of your soul. You can go through the motions of church activity and Christian talk but your heart is elsewhere. Whenever your heart's love and loyalty, which properly belongs to God, is directed towards something other than God, you have become what the Bible calls a "spiritual adulterer" (James 4:4–5). This makes you a friend of the world and, sadly, a functional enemy of God. As Jesus said, "No one can serve two masters. Either he will hate the one and love the other, or he will be devoted to the one and despise the other. You cannot serve both God and Money" (Matthew 6:24).

Most likely each of us will be tempted at some point to make money (and what we think it will provide for us) the functional source of our lives. This brings death, not life, to our relationship with God and others. Apart from going to Jesus in repentance and faith, all of our efforts to reform ourselves will fail. But with the knowledge of God's love for us in Christ and a turning to him for life, we will be liberated from bondage to our fears and our desires for what money provides. So we can budget, spend, and give with an open hand, as those who have security, meaning, validation, and pleasure in God himself. Hebrews 13:5–6 teaches:

> Keep your lives free from the love of money and be
> content with what you have, because God has said,
> "Never will I leave you; never will I forsake you."
> So we say with confidence, "The Lord is my helper;
> I will not be afraid. What can man do to me?"

Make this verse your everyday prayer, and God will answer you with a new contentment and the power to change both the way you view money and the purposes for which you spend money.

An Opportunity for a New Perspective on the Purpose of Money

Learning godly contentment will free you for another opportunity: to gain a new perspective on God's purpose for money. Paul shares this perspective in his first letter to Timothy. He begins by warning him not to make the pursuit of wealth a personal financial goal, but to be content with God. Paul, like Jesus, acknowledges the need for shelter, food, and clothing—the necessities of life (1 Timothy 6:6–10). In 1 Thessalonians 4:11–12, he adds to this thought, saying that, as followers of Christ, it should be our "ambition" to lead a quiet life, to pursue our calling and accomplish real work, so we may win the respect of outsiders and not be dependent on anyone else.

So it *is* God's will for us to work hard to provide ourselves and our families with life's necessities, but Paul doesn't stop there. He also says that the fundamental goal for our work is to have something to share with others. Instead of working hard to enhance our own lifestyles, Paul's revolutionary idea is that God's ultimate purpose for our work is to enable us to give to others. He explains this in his farewell to the Ephesians:

> You yourselves know that these hands of mine have supplied my own needs and the needs of my companions. In everything I did, I showed you that by this kind of hard work we must help the weak, remembering the words the Lord Jesus himself said: "It is more blessed to give than to receive." (Acts 20:34–35, see also Ephesians 4:28; 2 Thessalonians 3:10)

Paul is saying that the big picture of God's will for us financially is both profound and quite simple. The money God grants as a fruit of our labor is given that we might love our "neighbor" as we love ourselves. We work hard not only to provide for ourselves and our dependents, but also to help the weak, the lost, and the needy (Acts 20:34–35). This makes our work truly a labor of love.

Focusing only on providing for our families is like being a baseball player who is satisfied with getting to second base in a baseball game. It's great to get on base, but the goal is to score a run, not end the inning stranded on base. So it's great to provide for our families, but God has given us a greater goal for our money: loving our neighbors as ourselves. It is interesting that Christians who tithe ten percent of their income to God usually don't have a problem with overspending or excessive debt. Generous giving seems to self-adjust our choices and attitudes about money in the direction of spending control rooted in contentment.

Practical Strategies for Change

An Opportunity to Develop
Wise Spending Habits

When my wife and I had our financial crisis, I remember being irritated with her when our bank account hit zero. Since my wife paid the bills, I expected her to control spending for both of us. But when we sat down together to discover where all the money had gone, I was shocked to discover that, in one year, I was the one responsible for our overspending. Although I didn't realize it, my desire to possess was running quite a bit ahead of what God had provided. I was used to getting what I wanted in my upper middle-class upbringing, so how was I to downsize my expectations and my spending?

We asked God for help. We prayed that he would free us from our desire for a certain lifestyle and getting what we wanted. We asked him to teach us how to live within the financial boundaries he had given us and to be content. God answered those prayers by helping us develop a system of spending discipline that works well for not-so-organized folks like me. Following this plan helped us to make the spending changes we needed and to grow in contentment. God blessed our plea for help and our commitment to change, and within a few months we were living within our means, with a slight surplus.

Not all of our attempts to economize went smoothly. Our children still remember the homemade root beer blowing up in the basement, and our Volkswagen van breaking down on three consecutive trips (under Dad's engine-repair efforts). But even they were eventually glad for a family culture not based on spending. More deeply, however, it helped us learn to be satisfied with the basics God supplied. Our family began to learn that saying no to something does not result in the loss of anything essential to life.

If you are delinquent on your bills, but willing to take a faith-filled and fresh look at what it means to live within God's provision, let me encourage you to do the exercise that follows. It will give you an honest picture of your financial situation and show you what you need to do to bring your expenses in line with your income. It doesn't guarantee contentment, but it can (as it did for us) provide you with the opportunity to learn contentment, resulting in a life of financial realism, wisdom, and obedience.

Step One: Assess Your Financial Situation

Paul's advice to the Ephesians is to "be very careful then, how you live" in the light of the opportunities you have been given (Ephesians 5:15). Spending within the means of God's provision is part of that wisdom and submission to God.

Applied to your finances, it means that you must first determine the cause of your financial problems. Money problems can stem from either of two causes: not having enough money to provide necessities or overspending. While the stress can feel similar, the two situations require two different solutions. If you do not have enough for necessities, you need to earn more or make major structural changes to your cost of living. But it is possible that you are making enough money, but still falling behind on your bills every month. If that is true, the solution to your problem is learning how to control your spending. To find out which solution you need to apply, follow the exercise given below.

Start by gathering your financial information. The twelve bank statements from the previous year will likely be your most important documents. Go through those statements and do the following:

- Add your total deposits from all sources of income.
- Subtract from this total any deposits that were not income (like transfers into the account from savings, home-equity loans, or other loans), so you can determine your actual net income for the year.
- Add your total expenditures, including checks, ATM withdrawals, and electronic debits that were deducted from your bank account(s).
- Subtract your total expenses from your true income (figured in the first two steps of this exercise) to get your net gain or loss for the year.

If you are having problems paying your bills, then your expenses are most likely more than your income. This exercise will give you an estimate of how large your shortfall is. As difficult as it may be to face the facts, doing so is the precondition for a solution. So take this step by faith, remembering that you are God's child, your identity is not in how much money (or lack of it) you make, and he has promised to provide all your needs (Matthew 6:31–34). Facing your deficit without denial or terror requires an act of faith. It is the equivalent of professing dependence on God and praying, "Give us this day our daily bread."

Step Two: Plan Your Spending

After facing your deficit, it's time to create a spending plan for the next twelve months. If you are married, it is essential that your spouse fully participate. Without his or her cooperation, perspective, and accountability the system will be greatly weakened. To make a realistic plan for your spending, this is what you need to do:

Project your income. For employees this is fairly simple. You and your spouse's net paychecks can be added for the year's total. If you are self-employed, use last year's income as your guide to project the next year's income, based on past experience and current market conditions. Be sure to include interest, dividends, gifts, royalties, rental income, retirement income (if applicable), debt repayments, settlement payments, and tax refunds. Once this figure is determined, you should have a good estimate of total income available for the next year.

Project your expenses. Take another look at your expenses from the previous year. Gather as many of the checks, receipts, credit-card statements, monthly invoices, and bills from the previous year as you can find. Then make a list of the various categories of expenses and put them under one of two general headings (see the appendix for an example of an itemized list).

1. Fixed Expenses: Under this heading, list all expenses that are fixed by someone else (mortgage, utility bills, auto payment, insurance, etc.) or fixed by you (tithes to your church, savings plan, etc.).

2. Variable Expenses: Under this heading, list expenses you have some control over (groceries, eating out, gifts, vacations, clothing, etc.).

Between these two headings you should have a complete list of your expenses.

After you have listed your expenses under their appropriate headings, begin to plan your spending, adding numbers for each category (i.e. mortgage/rent, utilities, food, clothing, entertainment, etc.). Using the expenses from last year as a guide, project your spending for the next twelve months for each category of expenses. Be sure to use a twelve-month figure for planned spending because it will include bills that are paid annually or quarterly. Also, break down your ATM cash spending and your credit-card billings by identifying the actual items purchased. Assign each line in the credit-card bill to a category.

Once you have a projected dollar amount for each of the spending categories, add them and compare that amount with your total expected income for the next twelve months. It will probably be a loss, and it may be similar to your actual loss from the previous twelve months. But don't be discouraged when your first projections come out in the red. When my wife and I use this system, we often begin with a spending plan that is about ten to twenty percent more than our income, so we have to work hard to pare it down.

Why not start the process with prayer for God to guide you? God is sovereign in his assignment of your situation and loving in his intentions for you, so there is a way for you to move forward. As you seek God's will, his promise for wisdom will be worked in your own life (James 1:5–6). You can also enlist the prayers of others as you embark on this challenge of faith and stewardship.

Reconcile income and expenses. To begin, assume that all fixed expenses are going to be paid in full each month. That may leave a fairly small amount of money to be used for the variable expenses. Use your creativity to identify items you can eliminate or reduce. Consider eliminating cable television; canceling club memberships and magazine or newspaper subscriptions; eating meals at home and packing bag lunches instead of dining out; and shopping at thrift and discount stores.

Once you have a written estimation of how much you can reduce your expenses, add them again to see how much of the deficit you have eliminated. Cutting these costs is often not enough to do the job of balancing income and expenses. It is very common that some fixed expenses will need to be cut as well. Since 1970 the fixed costs faced by the average American family have risen from 54 percent to 75 percent of their total income.[2] This obviously leaves a smaller piece of the financial pie for discretionary spending.

If you cannot balance your budget through cutting variable expenses, go back through each category in the fixed list and look for ways you can reduce your structurally fixed expenses. Most of our large-dollar spending mistakes take place in the expenses we box ourselves into—primarily housing, auto, and debt payments. Consider relocating to a more affordable home or apartment, selling your second car (or both cars) and using public transportation, getting rid of your cell phone, and doing your own home repairs.

You can save money if you are willing to let go of your definition of "the good life," and commit yourself to living within the boundaries of God's provision for you in his goodness.

Seek help. After cutting both your variable and fixed expenses, if you still cannot operate on a positive cash-flow basis, you will need to seek some help. Often churches have financial counselors available. Ask your pastor, your elders, or your deacons for financial direction. If you are overwhelmed with debt payments to the point where you have no choice but to stop paying them, get credit counseling to seek debt-principal reductions. If that fails, consult an attorney about the possibility of filing for bankruptcy. Our modern bankruptcy laws were inspired by the Bible's provision for debts to be cancelled every seven years to give the indebted and poor a fresh start (see Leviticus 25).

Develop more income. You may also come to the conclusion that you are not earning enough to provide the everyday necessities for you and your family. In that case, you are called by God to seek to earn more income. This may mean starting the often painful and scary process of changing your vocation and perhaps retraining. As you face this reality, remember that you have a heavenly Father who cares for you and hears your prayers. When your life is built on God and his love for you, change doesn't have to be a threat; it can be an opportunity to see how God will lead you and provide for you. Do not "cave" until you are able to balance income and expenses on your worksheet.

Step Three: Put Yourself on an Allowance from Your Bank

Once you have balanced your income and expenses on paper, you can move to the next step of putting your spending plan into practice. While the key to controlling spending is a willingness to change your lifestyle to honor God, that willingness must be matched by a practical means of carrying it out. People often try complicated budgeting systems to control their spending, but these are hard to maintain. The following approach is for people who need limits on spending, but are not disciplined enough to budget or keep detailed records of where all the money goes. The heart of the system involves putting yourself on an allowance controlled by your bank account. This system will help you control your variable expenses, pay your bills on time, develop habits of saving and giving, and provide a reserve for unpredictable expenses.

Here's what you need to do:

1. Open a second bank account with **no** overdraft protection and no built-in credit line.

2. Continue to deposit all your income into your original checking account. From that account pay **only fixed expenses.** Do not pay for any items on the list of variable expenses from this account.

3. Twice each month, make a deposit (or transfer) from your original checking account into the new bank account. This deposit should be the amount equal to half of one month's variable spending.

4. Use **only** this new account to pay for items listed in your variable expenses. When the money in the account is used up, you will be **forced** to stop spending. You should wait until you make your next bi-monthly deposit from the fixed account before you spend on any other variable expenses.

5. If you have a long history of rigidly paying off credit-card charges each month you could keep using them; but if you are in credit-card debt, cut up your cards and get a debit card for each checking account.

6. Resist the temptation to pay variable bills with the fixed account funds.

7. Be accountable. Ask a deacon, elder, friend, spouse, or counselor to look at your bank statement each month, give advice, and pray with you.

8. After a year on this plan, if you have built up a surplus in the fixed account, transfer it to a savings account.

This system will help you take control of your personal finances. Once the debt has been paid off, you can begin to set more thoughtful long-term goals or adjust those goals to meet the expenses you envision in the future—children's college education, more adequate insurances, retirement investing, and increased giving.

Whether you live in plenty or want, trust God to help you live out Ephesians 5:15–17: "Be very careful, then, how you live—not as unwise but as wise, making the most of every opportunity, because the days are evil. Therefore do not be foolish, but understand what the Lord's will is." Stepping into God's will for your finances will fill you with a new contentment and joy as you find true life in God, whom to know is life indeed.

Endnotes

1 Sue Stock, "Money Talks," *Charlotte News and Observer*, May 6, 2007.

2 Rob Moll, "Scrooge Lives," Quotes Smith, Emerson, and Snell, *Passing the Plate* (Oxford: Oxford University Press, 2008), *Christianity Today*, December, 2008, 26.

Appendix

Below is a sample list of itemized expenses using the Fixed Expenses and Variable Expenses plan. You may adapt this list for your family's budget.

Fixed Expenses (for 12 months)	Variable Expenses (for 12 months)
Auto Fuel	Books, CD and DVDs
Auto Insurance	Cash Expenditures (not on this list)
Auto Loan	Clothing – Children
Auto Service (estimate)	Clothing – Husband
Auto Regist., Tags, Tolls, Misc.	Clothing – Wife
Bank Charges	Eating Out (including lunches)
Cell Phone	Entertainment (theatre, Netflix, etc.)
Child Support, Alimony	Gifts – Birthdays

Fixed Expenses (for 12 months)	Variable Expenses (for 12 months)
Church and Charitable Giving	Gifts – Christmas
Computer, Printer	Gifts – Other
Credit Card Debt	Groceries, Household Supplies
Credit Line Payments	Haircuts and Beauty Supplies
Dental Copays and Allowance	Hobby and Sports Expenses
Dental Insurance (if appl.)	Magazines and Newspapers
Income Taxes – Federal	Miscellaneous
Income Taxes – Local	Photos, Pictures
Income Taxes – State	Vacation and Travel
Insurance – Life	Other Variable Expenses
Insurance – Long-term Care	
Home – Heat and Electricity	
Home – Internet and Cable	
Home – Landscaping	

Fixed Expenses (for 12 months)	Variable Expenses (for 12 months)
Home – Maintenance Allowance	
Home – Mortgage or rental	
Home – Phone	
Home – Property Taxes	
Home – Repair Allowance	
Home – Water charges	
Homeowners' Association Fees	
Medical Copays	
Medical Insurance (if appl.)	
Pharmacy Copays	
Savings, IRA Contributions	
Other Fixed Expenses	
TOTAL	

Simple, Quick, Biblical

Advice on Complicated Counseling Issues for Pastors, Counselors, and Individuals

MINIBOOK
CATEGORIES

- Personal Change
- Marriage & Parenting
- Medical & Psychiatric Issues
- Women's Issues
- Singles
- Military

USE YOURSELF | GIVE TO A FRIEND | DISPLAY IN YOUR CHURCH OR MINIST

New Growth Press

Go to **www.newgrowthpress.com** or call **336.378.7775** to purchase individual minibooks or the entire collection. Durable acrylic display stands are also available to house the minibook collection.